Why Conspiracy Theories Are Dangerous

By James Hosie

1

Misinformation lies at the core of many conspiracy theories, serving as the fuel that propels these narratives. Conspiracy theories typically thrive on distorted or completely fabricated information, creating a distorted version of reality that adherents come to accept. There are several ways in which misinformation within conspiracy theories is particularly dangerous:

1. **Confirmation Bias:** Conspiracy theories often prey on individuals' existing beliefs and fears, exploiting confirmation

bias. People may be more inclined to accept information that aligns with their preconceived notions, even if it lacks credibility.

2. **Cherry-Picking Evidence:** Conspiracy theories often cherry-pick isolated pieces of information while ignoring the broader context or contradictory evidence. This selective presentation reinforces a skewed narrative that appears compelling but lacks a comprehensive foundation.

3. **Decontextualization:** Misinformation within conspiracy theories tends to thrive by

removing information from its original context. This can distort the meaning of events or statements, creating a misleading interpretation that supports the conspiracy narrative.

4. **Lack of Verifiable Sources:** Many conspiracy theories lack credible and verifiable sources. Instead, they rely on anonymous testimonies, unverified documents, or hearsay, making it challenging to fact-check and debunk the claims.

5. **Social Media Amplification:** The rise of social media has accelerated the

spread of misinformation. Conspiracy theories can gain rapid traction as they circulate through echo chambers, reaching a wide audience and reinforcing false beliefs.

6. **Distrust in Mainstream Media:** Conspiracy theorists often propagate the idea that mainstream media is part of the conspiracy, leading people to dismiss credible sources of information. This distrust further isolates individuals within their echo chambers.

7. **Creation of Echo Chambers:** Misinformation

fosters the formation of echo chambers, where like-minded individuals reinforce and validate each other's beliefs. This insular environment discourages critical thinking and openness to alternative perspectives.

8. **Impacts Public Discourse:** Widespread misinformation fueled by conspiracy theories can significantly impact public discourse. Debates on critical issues become polarized, making it difficult to have informed discussions based on accurate information.

9. **Undermines Scientific Consensus:** Conspiracy theories often challenge well-established scientific principles. This not only misguides public understanding but also undermines the credibility of scientific consensus, hindering evidence-based decision-making.

10. **Harms Public Trust:** The reliance on misinformation erodes public trust in information sources, contributing to a broader atmosphere of skepticism and confusion. This can have far-reaching consequences, from political decision-making to public health initiatives, as people

may be hesitant to trust authoritative guidance.

2

Undermining trust is a significant and far-reaching consequence of widespread belief in conspiracy theories. When individuals embrace conspiratorial narratives, it often translates into a broader erosion of trust in key societal institutions, with profound implications for social cohesion and stability. Here are several ways in which the belief in conspiracies can undermine trust:

1. **Distrust in Government:** Conspiracy theories frequently target government institutions, painting them as malevolent actors involved in secretive and harmful activities. This can lead to a pervasive distrust in government, hindering the effectiveness of public policies and eroding confidence in political leadership.

2. **Skepticism Toward Scientific Authorities:** Conspiracies often challenge scientific consensus, fostering skepticism toward established scientific principles. This not only impedes progress in areas such as

public health but also erodes public trust in scientific authorities and research institutions.

3. **Media Mistrust:** Conspiracy theories often depict mainstream media as complicit in covering up supposed conspiracies. This contributes to a general mistrust in media outlets, making it challenging for the public to differentiate between credible journalism and misinformation.

4. **Weakening Social Cohesion:** Trust in institutions is foundational to social cohesion.

When conspiracy theories undermine this trust, it can fragment society, fostering a sense of alienation and disconnection among different groups with conflicting beliefs.

5. **Polarization and Division:** Belief in conspiracies tends to foster an "us versus them" mentality, creating ideological divisions within society. This polarization makes it difficult for individuals to find common ground, hindering constructive dialogue and collaboration.

6. **Erosion of Democratic Processes:** When a significant

portion of the population distrusts the electoral process due to conspiratorial beliefs, it can lead to a lack of faith in democratic institutions. This can undermine the legitimacy of elected officials and democratic processes, posing a threat to the stability of the political system.

7. **Impact on Social Institutions:** Institutions such as law enforcement, educational systems, and healthcare may face challenges when conspiracy theories circulate. Public skepticism can hinder the ability of these institutions to carry out their functions effectively.

8. **Resistance to Authority:** The erosion of trust may result in resistance to authority, making it challenging for institutions to implement necessary measures or respond to crises effectively. This resistance can impede efforts to address issues ranging from public health emergencies to national security threats.

9. **Psychological Impact:** The pervasive distrust associated with conspiracy beliefs can have a psychological impact on individuals, fostering a general sense of anxiety and paranoia. This can further contribute to

societal instability as people become more suspicious and less cooperative.

10. **Reduced Civic Engagement:** When trust in institutions diminishes, individuals may become less likely to engage in civic activities such as voting, community participation, or activism. This reduction in civic engagement can undermine the democratic functioning of society.

3

Divisiveness is a notable consequence of the proliferation

of conspiracy theories, as these narratives often contribute to the creation of sharp divides within society. The "us versus them" mentality fostered by conspiracy beliefs can hinder constructive dialogue and cooperation, leading to a range of social challenges. Here are several ways in which conspiracy theories contribute to divisiveness:

1. **Group Polarization:** Conspiracy theories tend to create or exacerbate existing ideological divides by aligning individuals with specific beliefs. This polarization reinforces the idea that there are distinct groups of

"believers" versus "non-believers," leading to a breakdown of nuanced discussions.

2. **Social Fragmentation:** Conspiracy theories often promote the notion that certain groups or institutions are working against the common good. This can lead to social fragmentation, with individuals distancing themselves from those who hold differing beliefs, eroding the sense of a shared societal identity.

3. **In-Group versus Out-Group Dynamics:** Belief in conspiracy theories can create an in-

group/out-group dynamic, where individuals who share similar beliefs form a cohesive in-group, viewing those who disagree as outsiders or adversaries. This dynamic heightens social tension and diminishes empathy across different groups.

4. **Erosion of Trust in Relationships:** Friendships, families, and communities can be strained or even fractured when conspiracy beliefs take hold. Trust within these social units may erode as individuals become entrenched in their beliefs, viewing dissenting opinions as a threat.

5. **Stigmatization and Marginalization:** Conspiracies often target specific individuals or groups as the supposed orchestrators of malevolent schemes. This can lead to the stigmatization and marginalization of those falsely implicated, exacerbating societal divisions and fostering discrimination.

6. **Political Polarization:** Conspiracy theories can become intertwined with political ideologies, contributing to the polarization of political discourse. This polarization makes it

challenging for people to find common ground, hindering the compromise necessary for effective governance.

7. **Obstruction of Constructive Dialogue:** The "us versus them" mentality promoted by conspiracy theories obstructs open and constructive dialogue. When individuals are entrenched in their beliefs, meaningful conversation becomes difficult, hindering the exchange of ideas and the search for common ground.

8. **Reduced Social Cohesion:** Divisiveness fueled by conspiracy theories weakens the fabric of

social cohesion. A society marked by deep divisions is less likely to collaborate on shared goals and may struggle to address collective challenges effectively.

9. **Cultural and Ethnic Tensions:** Some conspiracy theories involve cultural or ethnic stereotypes and prejudices, intensifying tensions among diverse groups. This can contribute to discriminatory behaviors and heighten existing cultural and ethnic divides.

10. **Resilience to Factual Information:** Once individuals adopt a conspiratorial mindset,

they may become resistant to factual information that contradicts their beliefs. This resistance further deepens the divisions by impeding the possibility of shared understanding based on accurate information.

4

The dissemination of conspiracy theories can have severe consequences for the reputation of individuals or groups who find themselves falsely implicated in these narratives. The harm to reputation is not merely a matter of personal perception; it can have tangible impacts on the lives and livelihoods of those targeted. Here are several ways in which conspiracy theories can cause harm to reputation:

1. **Character Assassination:** Conspiracy theories often involve accusations of malicious intent or involvement in secretive, harmful activities. Individuals or groups falsely implicated may face character assassination as their motives, ethics, and integrity are called into question without basis.

2. **Professional Consequences:** Reputational damage from conspiracy theories

can have significant professional repercussions. Individuals may experience difficulty finding employment, maintaining existing roles, or advancing in their careers as a result of unfounded suspicions and negative perceptions.

3. **Social Stigmatization:** Falsely being associated with a conspiracy can lead to social stigmatization. Friends, colleagues, and community members may distance themselves, believing the false accusations and contributing to a sense of isolation for the targeted individuals or groups.

4. **Loss of Opportunities:** Reputational damage can result in missed opportunities for personal and professional growth. Individuals may lose out on educational, career, or social opportunities due to the unfounded suspicions created by conspiracy theories.

5. **Legal Ramifications:** In extreme cases, false accusations in conspiracy theories can lead to legal consequences. Individuals may face baseless legal challenges, investigations, or lawsuits, adding a layer of stress

and financial burden to the reputational harm.

6. **Financial Impact:** A damaged reputation can affect financial stability. Businesses associated with individuals targeted by conspiracy theories may suffer a decline in sales or partnerships, impacting the economic well-being of those involved.

7. **Psychological Toll:** The psychological toll of being falsely implicated in a conspiracy can be profound. The stress, anxiety, and emotional distress resulting from reputational damage can impact

an individual's overall well-being and mental health.

8. **Family and Relationship Strain:** False accusations can strain relationships with family and friends, causing rifts that may be challenging to repair. The impact extends beyond the individual, affecting the broader network of those associated with the targeted person or group.

9. **Difficulty Rebuilding Trust:** Even if the conspiracy theories are debunked, rebuilding trust can be a formidable task. The stigma associated with false accusations may persist, making it

challenging for individuals to regain the trust of colleagues, friends, and the public.

10. **Long-Term Impact on Legacy:** Reputational harm can have a lasting impact on an individual's legacy. False accusations may overshadow genuine achievements and contributions, tarnishing a person's reputation in the eyes of future generations.

In summary, the harm to reputation resulting from false implications in conspiracy theories extends beyond personal perception, affecting various aspects of individuals' lives and leaving enduring consequences. The social, professional, and psychological impacts can be substantial and may persist long after the conspiracy theories are debunked.

5

Conspiracy theories, particularly those related to public health issues such as vaccines, pose significant risks to public health efforts. When misinformation spreads, especially in the context of vaccination, it can undermine trust in vaccines and the healthcare system, leading to a range of consequences that jeopardize the well-being of communities. Here are several ways in which conspiracy theories contribute to public health risks, particularly in the context of vaccine hesitancy:

1. **Reduced Vaccination Rates:** Conspiracy theories often cast doubt on the safety and efficacy of vaccines, leading to increased vaccine hesitancy. This can result in lower vaccination rates within communities, leaving populations vulnerable to preventable diseases.

2. **Resurgence of Preventable Diseases:** A decline in vaccination rates due to hesitancy fueled by conspiracy theories can lead to the resurgence of preventable diseases. Diseases once under control, such as measles or whooping cough, may experience outbreaks, putting individuals, especially vulnerable populations like children and the immunocompromised, at risk.

3. **Compromised Herd Immunity:** Herd immunity, achieved when a significant portion of a population is immune to a disease, is crucial for protecting those who cannot be

vaccinated. Conspiracy-driven vaccine hesitancy undermines herd immunity, allowing diseases to circulate more freely within communities.

4. **Delayed or Missed Immunizations:** Individuals influenced by vaccine conspiracy theories may delay or forgo immunizations for themselves or their children. This delay increases the window of susceptibility to diseases, making it more challenging to control the spread of infectious agents.

5. **Increased Healthcare Costs:** Outbreaks of preventable

diseases strain healthcare systems, leading to increased medical costs. Treating vaccine-preventable illnesses and managing outbreaks demands resources that could otherwise be allocated to other healthcare priorities.

6. **Impact on Global Health Initiatives:** Vaccine hesitancy driven by conspiracy theories not only affects local communities but also hampers global health efforts. International vaccination campaigns and initiatives may face challenges when confronted with widespread distrust in vaccines.

7. **Disruption of Disease Eradication Programs:** In the case of diseases targeted for eradication, such as polio, conspiracy-driven vaccine hesitancy can disrupt global efforts to eliminate the disease. This prolongs the time and resources needed to achieve eradication goals.

8. **Spread of Misinformation:** Conspiracy theories often rely on misinformation about vaccine ingredients, safety, and side effects. This misinformation spreads easily through social media and other channels,

contributing to a climate of confusion and fear surrounding vaccines.

9. **Public Anxiety and Fear:** Conspiracy-driven vaccine hesitancy can create an environment of anxiety and fear regarding vaccination. This fear can deter individuals from seeking essential healthcare services and trusting medical professionals, leading to broader public health challenges.

10. **Erosion of Trust in Health Authorities:** The spread of vaccine-related conspiracy theories erodes trust in health

authorities and medical professionals. This lack of trust can hinder public health communication efforts and diminish the effectiveness of vaccination campaigns.

In summary, conspiracy theories related to vaccines can have profound implications for public health. They undermine vaccination efforts, compromise herd immunity, and pose risks to individuals and communities by facilitating the resurgence of preventable diseases. Addressing vaccine hesitancy requires targeted public health communication, education, and efforts to counteract misinformation.

6

The intersection between conspiracy theories and radicalization is a concerning phenomenon that can have serious implications for national security. Extreme conspiracy beliefs, when embraced by individuals or groups, can contribute to radicalization and the adoption of extremist ideologies. Here's how conspiracy theories can fuel radicalization and pose risks to national security:

1. **Creation of Enemy Narratives:** Conspiracy theories often involve the creation of narratives where certain groups or institutions are portrayed as malevolent forces conspiring against society. This narrative can contribute to the identification of perceived enemies, fostering a "us versus them" mentality that fuels extremist ideologies.

2. **Justification for Violence:** Some conspiracy theories provide a justification for violence, portraying it as a necessary response to perceived threats. Individuals radicalized through these beliefs may view violence as

a legitimate means to address imagined conspiracies, posing a direct threat to national security.

3. **Cultivation of Paranoia and Distrust:** Extreme conspiracy beliefs cultivate paranoia and deep-seated distrust in societal institutions. This distrust can drive individuals toward radical ideologies that promise a sense of belonging and purpose, often rooted in the idea of fighting against imagined conspirators.

4. **Recruitment Tool:** Extremist groups may exploit existing conspiracy theories as recruitment tools. By tapping into

individuals' pre-existing suspicions and fears, these groups can lure people into their ranks, offering a sense of community and purpose in the fight against perceived conspiracies.

5. **Destabilization of Societal Harmony:** Conspiracy-driven radicalization can contribute to social divisions and strife. When individuals become radicalized based on unfounded beliefs, it can lead to acts of violence, protests, or other disruptions that destabilize the fabric of society.

6. **Convergence of Beliefs:** Extremist ideologies and

conspiracy theories sometimes converge, reinforcing each other. This convergence can create a potent ideological cocktail that fuels radicalization, making individuals more susceptible to engaging in violent actions.

7. **Undermining Social Cohesion:** The radicalization fueled by extreme conspiracy beliefs undermines social cohesion. As individuals become more entrenched in their radicalized ideologies, they may distance themselves from mainstream society, hindering efforts to maintain unity and cooperation.

8. **Cybersecurity Threats:** Some conspiracy-driven radicalization may manifest in cyber threats. Individuals radicalized through these beliefs may engage in hacking, disinformation campaigns, or other cyber activities that pose risks to national security and critical infrastructure.

9. **Acts of Terrorism:** In the most severe cases, individuals radicalized by extreme conspiracy beliefs may carry out acts of terrorism. These acts can result in loss of life, damage to infrastructure, and a broader

impact on the nation's security landscape.

10. **Challenges for Law Enforcement:** Identifying and addressing radicalization based on conspiracy theories presents challenges for law enforcement. The clandestine nature of many extremist groups and the diffuse online spaces where radicalization occurs make it difficult to monitor and prevent potential threats.

Addressing the intersection of conspiracy theories and radicalization requires a multifaceted approach involving education, countering misinformation, and promoting critical thinking. It also involves efforts to strengthen social cohesion, address systemic issues that contribute to radicalization, and enhance intelligence and law enforcement capabilities to mitigate national security risks.

7

Distrust in authorities, often fueled by conspiracy theories and a general atmosphere of suspicion, can have significant repercussions for the effective functioning of institutions and hinder their ability to address real issues. Here's how constant suspicion and distrust can undermine the effectiveness of authorities:

1. **Diminished Legitimacy:** Constant suspicion erodes the perceived legitimacy of authorities. When people distrust those in positions of power, they may question the legitimacy of government actions, policies, and decisions, hindering the public's willingness to comply with laws and regulations.

2. **Impaired Crisis Response:** In times of crisis, whether it be a natural disaster, public health emergency, or security threat, effective response from

authorities is crucial. Distrust can lead to skepticism about the severity of the crisis or the appropriateness of response measures, potentially delaying or hindering necessary interventions.

3. **Undermining Public Health Initiatives:** During health crises, such as pandemics, distrust in health authorities can lead to skepticism about the efficacy and safety of public health measures, like vaccination campaigns. This skepticism can hinder efforts to control the spread of diseases and protect public health.

4. **Reduced Cooperation with Law Enforcement:** Distrust in law enforcement agencies can lead to reduced cooperation from the public. Individuals may be hesitant to report crimes, provide information, or collaborate with authorities, hindering efforts to maintain public safety.

5. **Challenges in Policy Implementation:** Authorities rely on public cooperation to implement and enforce policies effectively. Distrust can lead to non-compliance and resistance, making it challenging for authorities to implement policies that address real societal issues,

from environmental concerns to social welfare programs.

6. **Erosion of Democratic Processes:** Distrust in political institutions can undermine democratic processes. Citizens may be less likely to participate in elections, engage in civic activities, or trust the outcomes of democratic decision-making, weakening the foundations of a democratic society.

7. **Ineffective Communication:** Distrust can lead to a breakdown in communication between authorities and the public. When

there is a lack of trust, messages from authorities may be met with skepticism, making it difficult to convey important information and instructions.

8. **Conspiracy Theory Amplification:** Distrust often provides fertile ground for the spread of conspiracy theories. Individuals who mistrust authorities may be more susceptible to alternative narratives, even those lacking factual basis, further undermining the public's understanding of real issues.

9. **Social Fragmentation:** Widespread distrust can contribute to social fragmentation. Communities may become divided along lines of trust and distrust, hindering collective action and cooperation on issues that require a unified effort.

10. **Loss of Confidence in Institutions:** Persistent distrust erodes confidence in public institutions, from government bodies to regulatory agencies. This loss of confidence can have long-lasting consequences, as rebuilding trust in institutions is often a complex and time-consuming process.

Addressing distrust in authorities requires proactive efforts to foster transparency, accountability, and open communication. Building public trust is essential for effective governance, crisis response, and the successful implementation of policies aimed at addressing real societal challenges.

8

The connection between conspiracy theories and violence or social unrest is a significant concern, as certain narratives can inspire individuals or groups to act in ways that pose tangible threats to communities. Here's how conspiracy theories can fuel violence and social unrest, impacting the safety and stability of societies:

1. **Mobilization of Extremist Groups:** Some conspiracy theories become rallying points for extremist groups seeking a cause to champion. These groups may interpret conspiracy narratives as a call to action, mobilizing their members to engage in violent activities with the perceived aim of addressing the imagined threats outlined in the conspiracy.

2. **Radicalization of Individuals:** Conspiracy theories can contribute to the radicalization of individuals who come to believe that violence is a justifiable response to perceived threats. Individuals may act on these beliefs, carrying out acts of violence against perceived enemies or those associated with the supposed conspiracies.

3. **Targeting Specific Groups:** Certain conspiracy theories target specific individuals or groups, labeling them as enemies or threats to society. This can lead to violence and

discrimination against those falsely implicated, contributing to social unrest and harming the targeted individuals or communities.

4. **Acts of Terrorism:** In extreme cases, individuals or groups radicalized by conspiracy theories may resort to acts of terrorism. These acts can range from targeted violence against specific individuals to larger-scale attacks with the aim of causing fear and disruption within a community or society.

5. **Protests and Demonstrations:** Conspiracy-

driven beliefs can motivate individuals to participate in protests and demonstrations, sometimes escalating to violence. These events may be fueled by a sense of grievance or a desire to resist perceived conspiracies, leading to clashes with law enforcement or opposing groups.

6. **Weaponization of Information:** The spread of conspiracy theories through various channels, including social media, can contribute to the weaponization of information. False narratives may be used to justify violence, recruit supporters, or incite unrest,

amplifying the potential for real-world harm.

7. **Destabilization of Social Order:** Conspiracy-driven violence can destabilize the social order by creating an atmosphere of fear and uncertainty. This can lead to a breakdown in community cohesion, hindering normal day-to-day activities and fostering an environment conducive to further violence and unrest.

8. **Impact on Public Safety:** Acts of violence inspired by conspiracy theories pose direct threats to public safety.

Individuals or communities targeted by such violence may experience lasting trauma, and the overall sense of security within society may be compromised.

9. **Challenges for Law Enforcement:** Addressing violence fueled by conspiracy theories presents challenges for law enforcement. Identifying and mitigating threats may be complicated by the clandestine nature of extremist groups and the diffusion of radicalization through online platforms.

10. **Polarization and Division:** Conspiracy theories

can contribute to polarization within society. As individuals become entrenched in their beliefs, divisions may deepen, making it more difficult to find common ground and fostering an environment where violence and unrest are more likely to occur.

Addressing the nexus between conspiracy theories and violence requires a comprehensive approach that involves countering misinformation, promoting critical thinking, and addressing underlying social, economic, and political factors that contribute to radicalization and social unrest. It also necessitates effective law enforcement strategies to prevent and respond to violence inspired by conspiracy-driven ideologies.

9

Conspiracy theories, with their focus on imagined or exaggerated threats, have the potential to divert attention and resources away from addressing real problems that demand thoughtful solutions. Here's how the preoccupation with conspiracy theories can lead to ineffective problem-solving:

1. **Misallocation of Resources:** When attention is

directed towards addressing perceived conspiracies or imagined threats, resources that could be better utilized to tackle actual issues may be misallocated. This misallocation hinders the effective allocation of funds, time, and efforts to address genuine problems.

2. **Neglect of Public Health Issues:** Conspiracy theories, especially those related to health, can divert attention from critical public health concerns. For example, during a global pandemic, a focus on misinformation and conspiracy narratives can distract from the

urgent need to address and mitigate the real health crisis at hand.

3. **Undermining Environmental Efforts:** Some conspiracy theories undermine efforts to address environmental challenges by casting doubt on the validity of scientific evidence. This can lead to a delay in implementing necessary policies and actions to combat climate change, deforestation, or pollution.

4. **Erosion of Trust in Scientific Solutions:** Conspiracy theories that target scientific advancements or technologies can erode public

trust in innovative solutions to real problems. This distrust may impede the adoption of beneficial technologies and slow down progress in areas such as medicine, renewable energy, and environmental conservation.

5. **Political Distractions:** Conspiracy theories often thrive in political arenas, diverting attention from pressing political issues. In the realm of governance, the focus on perceived conspiracies may detract from addressing economic inequality, social justice, or geopolitical challenges that

require concerted efforts and solutions.

6. **Delay in Crisis Response:** The diversion of attention to imagined threats can lead to delays in responding to actual crises. Whether it be a natural disaster, a public health emergency, or a security threat, effective problem-solving requires timely and focused responses that may be hindered by the distraction of conspiracy narratives.

7. **Hindrance to Social Progress:** By fostering skepticism and resistance to change, conspiracy theories can

hinder social progress. This resistance may impede advancements in civil rights, gender equality, and other areas where positive societal changes are needed.

8. **Obstruction of Scientific Research:** Conspiracy theories that question the legitimacy of scientific research can hinder the progress of studies aimed at understanding and solving real-world problems. This obstruction may impede breakthroughs in areas like medicine, technology, and environmental science.

9. **Creation of Unnecessary Fears:** Imagined threats propagated by conspiracy theories can create unnecessary fears among the public. This fear may divert attention from genuine issues and lead to unwarranted anxiety, making it difficult for individuals and communities to focus on pragmatic solutions.

10. **Undermining Social Cohesion:** Conspiracy theories that perpetuate divisions within society can undermine social cohesion. When communities are divided along ideological lines, collective efforts to solve shared problems become more

challenging, hindering the potential for collaborative solutions.

To address these challenges, fostering critical thinking, promoting media literacy, and emphasizing evidence-based decision-making are crucial. Encouraging a focus on real problems, supported by accurate information and sound reasoning, is essential for effective problem-solving and societal progress.

10

Belief in certain conspiracy theories has the potential to

discourage individuals and communities from actively participating in scientific advancements and societal progress. This skepticism can impede overall development by hindering innovation, eroding trust in institutions, and fostering an atmosphere of doubt and resistance. Here's how belief in conspiracies can stifle progress:

1. **Resistance to Scientific Innovation:** Conspiracy theories that target scientific advancements, especially in fields like medicine and technology, can create resistance to adopting new innovations. Individuals may be

hesitant to embrace breakthroughs, leading to delays in the application of beneficial technologies and hindering advancements that could improve quality of life.

2. **Public Health Consequences:** Conspiracy theories related to healthcare, such as vaccine hesitancy, can have significant public health consequences. The resistance to proven medical interventions can contribute to the persistence of preventable diseases, compromise community immunity, and impede efforts to address global health challenges.

3. **Undermining Trust in Institutions:** Belief in certain conspiracies often involves a deep-seated distrust in scientific institutions, government agencies, and other entities responsible for societal progress. This erosion of trust can hinder collaboration and coordination, essential elements for addressing complex issues that require collective efforts.

4. **Spread of Misinformation:** Conspiracy theories often thrive on the spread of misinformation. When individuals believe in false narratives, they may resist information that contradicts their

conspiratorial views. This resistance impedes the dissemination of accurate information, hindering the public's understanding of critical issues.

5. **Dampening Innovation and Entrepreneurship:** Skepticism toward scientific and technological advancements can deter individuals from pursuing careers in innovative fields. The fear of being associated with perceived conspiracies may stifle entrepreneurship and innovation, slowing down progress in areas like technology, renewable energy, and biotechnology.

6. **Delay in Policy Implementation:** Conspiracy-driven resistance to certain policies, such as environmental regulations or public health measures, can lead to delays in their implementation. This delay can have far-reaching consequences for addressing urgent societal challenges, from climate change to infectious disease control.

7. **Threat to Global Cooperation:** Belief in global conspiracy theories may undermine international cooperation. Collaboration between countries and

organizations is crucial for addressing issues like climate change, global health crises, and economic disparities. Conspiracy-driven skepticism may hinder effective collaboration on these global challenges.

8. **Erosion of Intellectual Curiosity:** Conspiracy theories can discourage intellectual curiosity by fostering a mindset that distrusts information coming from established sources. This erosion of curiosity may hinder educational pursuits, critical thinking, and the exploration of new ideas essential for societal advancement.

9. **Challenges to Evidence-Based Decision-Making:** Scientific progress relies on evidence-based decision-making. Belief in certain conspiracies, which often lack a basis in credible evidence, can lead to decisions that are not grounded in reality. This challenges the effectiveness of policies and initiatives aimed at societal improvement.

10. **Impact on Education:** Conspiracy theories can influence educational attitudes and choices. Individuals who believe in certain conspiracies may be less inclined

to pursue education in science, technology, engineering, and mathematics (STEM) fields, limiting the pool of talent and expertise crucial for driving innovation and progress.

Addressing the stifling effects of conspiracy beliefs on progress requires efforts to promote science literacy, critical thinking skills, and open dialogue. Fostering a culture that values evidence-based decision-making and encourages curiosity is essential for overcoming the barriers created by conspiratorial thinking.

11

The erosion of critical thinking is a significant consequence associated with the proliferation of conspiracy theories. These theories often discourage individuals from engaging in rigorous and objective analysis of evidence, leading to uncritical acceptance of unverified claims. Here's how the spread of conspiracy theories can contribute to the erosion of critical thinking:

1. **Selective Acceptance of Evidence:** Conspiracy theories often present a selective interpretation of evidence,

focusing on information that supports the narrative while disregarding contradictory evidence. This selective acceptance can create a skewed perception of reality, hindering individuals from considering a comprehensive range of information.

2. **Confirmation Bias Reinforcement:** Conspiracy theories thrive on confirmation bias, where individuals are more likely to accept information that aligns with their existing beliefs. This reinforcement of confirmation bias discourages critical examination of alternative

viewpoints and contributes to the entrenchment of conspiratorial thinking.

3. **Cherry-Picking Data:** Conspiracy theories often cherry-pick data points or incidents to construct a narrative that supports the conspiracy. This method of presenting information out of context or selectively can mislead individuals and hinder their ability to critically assess the overall validity of the claims.

4. **Appeal to Emotions over Evidence:** Many conspiracy theories leverage emotional appeal rather than relying on

verifiable evidence. Appeals to fear, mistrust, or anger can cloud individuals' judgment, making them more susceptible to accepting claims without scrutinizing the evidence supporting those claims.

5. **Dismissal of Expertise:** Conspiracies often involve the dismissal of expert opinions and established knowledge. Individuals may be discouraged from consulting credible sources or experts, leading to the rejection of well-established scientific, historical, or factual information critical for informed decision-making.

6. **False Equivalencies:** Conspiracy theories often create false equivalencies between well-supported evidence and unfounded claims. This blurring of distinctions between credible information and baseless assertions undermines the ability to discern the reliability of different sources.

7. **Encouragement of Anecdotal Evidence:** Conspiracy theories frequently rely on anecdotal evidence, personal testimonials, or unverified accounts rather than robust empirical evidence. This reliance on anecdotal information

can lead individuals to accept claims without demanding the rigor of scientifically validated evidence.

8. **Rejection of Skepticism:** Conspiracies may discourage skepticism by portraying those who question the narrative as part of the alleged conspiracy. This discouragement of healthy skepticism undermines the scientific method and critical inquiry essential for distinguishing fact from fiction.

9. **Cultivation of Paranoia:** Some conspiracy theories foster a culture of paranoia, where

individuals become overly suspicious of mainstream information sources. This heightened suspicion can hinder open-minded and critical engagement with diverse perspectives and reliable information.

10. **Isolation within Echo Chambers:** The prevalence of conspiracy theories can create echo chambers, where individuals are surrounded by like-minded individuals who reinforce and validate conspiratorial beliefs. This isolation limits exposure to diverse viewpoints and impedes

the development of critical thinking skills.

Addressing the erosion of critical thinking in the context of conspiracy theories requires educational efforts that emphasize media literacy, critical analysis skills, and the importance of evidence-based reasoning. Encouraging a culture of open-minded inquiry and skepticism in the face of extraordinary claims is essential for fostering a society that values critical thinking.

The normalization of distrust, fueled by widespread acceptance of conspiracy theories, has profound implications for informed decision-making within society. As conspiracy narratives become more prevalent and influential, they contribute to a broader culture of skepticism and mistrust toward information sources. Here's how the normalization of distrust impedes the ability to make informed decisions:

1. **Undermining Credible Information Sources:** Conspiracy theories often cast doubt on traditionally reliable

sources of information, such as mainstream media, scientific institutions, and government agencies. This erosion of trust makes it challenging for individuals to discern between credible and unreliable information, hindering their ability to make informed decisions.

2. **Proliferation of Alternative Narratives:** The normalization of distrust encourages the proliferation of alternative narratives that may lack empirical evidence or factual basis. Individuals may turn to alternative sources that align with their

existing beliefs, further limiting exposure to diverse perspectives and comprehensive information.

3. **Crisis of Authority:** Widespread acceptance of conspiracy theories contributes to a crisis of authority, where institutions and figures traditionally seen as authoritative sources of information lose credibility. This crisis can lead to confusion and uncertainty, making it difficult for individuals to identify trustworthy sources when seeking information.

4. **Compromised Public Discourse:** A culture of

normalized distrust hampers constructive public discourse. When individuals question the legitimacy of information sources, meaningful dialogue becomes challenging, hindering the exchange of ideas and collaborative problem-solving.

5. **Erosion of Social Cohesion:** The normalization of distrust contributes to social fragmentation, as individuals become more skeptical of information presented by others. This erosion of social cohesion makes it difficult to build consensus and address shared challenges effectively.

6. **Paralysis in Decision-Making:** The prevalence of conspiracy theories can lead to decision-making paralysis, as individuals may hesitate to act on information they perceive as untrustworthy. This hesitation can impede timely responses to important issues, from public health emergencies to environmental crises.

7. **Propagation of Disinformation:** The normalization of distrust creates an environment conducive to the spread of disinformation. Individuals may be more

susceptible to accepting and sharing unverified claims, contributing to the amplification of false narratives and hindering efforts to combat misinformation.

8. **Weakening Democratic Processes:** In a democratic society, trust in information sources is essential for informed voting and civic engagement. The normalization of distrust weakens democratic processes, as citizens may become disillusioned and disengaged from the political system.

9. **Erosion of Confidence in Institutions:** Institutions that are

crucial for societal functioning, such as government bodies and scientific organizations, may face erosion of public confidence. The normalization of distrust can lead to decreased support for policies and initiatives that are essential for addressing societal challenges.

10. **Challenges in Crisis Management:** During crises, the normalization of distrust poses challenges for crisis management. Authorities may face difficulties in disseminating accurate and timely information, leading to confusion and potential delays in implementing effective response measures.

Addressing the normalization of distrust requires comprehensive efforts to promote media literacy, critical thinking, and a culture of open-minded inquiry. Building resilience against the influence of conspiracy theories involves fostering a society that values evidence-based reasoning and actively engages with diverse, reliable information sources.

13

Scapegoating is a disturbing consequence of certain conspiracy theories, wherein specific groups or individuals are unfairly targeted as the supposed orchestrators of malevolent schemes. The impact of scapegoating can extend beyond the realm of conspiracy theories, contributing to discrimination, prejudice, and harm to innocent individuals or communities. Here's how scapegoating manifests and its detrimental effects:

1. **Creation of Bogus Narratives:** Conspiracy theories often involve the creation of elaborate, often baseless narratives that cast blame on specific groups or individuals for imagined wrongdoing. These

narratives may include stereotypes, prejudices, and unfounded accusations that contribute to the scapegoating of the targeted entities.

2. **Fanning the Flames of Prejudice:** Scapegoating amplifies existing prejudices and biases. Conspiracy theories that single out particular groups as malevolent actors can reinforce negative stereotypes, fostering an environment where discrimination and bias are more likely to occur.

3. **Marginalization and Stigmatization:** Scapegoating can lead to the marginalization

and stigmatization of the targeted groups or individuals. Those falsely implicated in conspiracy theories may experience isolation, social exclusion, and heightened scrutiny, damaging their personal and community well-being.

4. **Erosion of Social Cohesion:** The unjust scapegoating promoted by conspiracy theories contributes to the erosion of social cohesion. When specific groups are unfairly blamed for perceived societal ills, it creates division, mistrust, and tension within communities, hindering the development of a

shared sense of identity and purpose.

5. **Fueling Discriminatory Practices:** Scapegoating can fuel discriminatory practices, ranging from social exclusion to systemic discrimination. Individuals and groups targeted by conspiracy theories may face challenges in areas such as employment, education, and healthcare due to the unfounded suspicions propagated by these narratives.

6. **Perpetuation of Inequality:** Conspiracy-driven scapegoating often perpetuates existing social

inequalities. Targeted groups may already face systemic disadvantages, and the additional burden of being unfairly scapegoated exacerbates these disparities, hindering efforts toward a more equitable society.

7. **Risk of Hate Crimes:** In extreme cases, scapegoating can contribute to the risk of hate crimes. Individuals or groups falsely implicated in conspiracy theories may become the targets of violence, harassment, or other harmful actions fueled by the baseless accusations.

8. **Division within Communities:** Scapegoating contributes to division within communities. When conspiracy theories pit different groups against each other, it hinders the potential for collaboration, dialogue, and mutual understanding, fostering a fractured social landscape.

9. **Impact on Mental Health:** The individuals or communities unfairly targeted by scapegoating may experience significant mental health challenges. The stress, anxiety, and trauma resulting from discrimination and stigmatization

can have long-lasting effects on the well-being of those affected.

10. **Normalization of Discrimination:** Scapegoating, when perpetuated by conspiracy theories, normalizes discriminatory attitudes within society. It can contribute to a culture where unjust accusations and prejudices are accepted, making it more challenging to address broader issues of social justice and equality.

Addressing the harmful impact of scapegoating necessitates efforts to debunk unfounded conspiracy theories, promote media literacy, and foster a culture of empathy, inclusivity, and critical thinking. Combating discrimination requires collective awareness and action to dismantle the stereotypes and biases perpetuated by conspiracy-driven scapegoating.

14

Belief in conspiracy theories during crises can impair effective crisis response efforts, introducing challenges that hinder the ability to manage and mitigate the impact of emergencies. Here's how the prevalence of conspiracy theories can interfere with crisis response:

1. **Panic and Fear:** Conspiracy theories often thrive on fear-inducing narratives, and during a crisis, these narratives can contribute to widespread panic. Belief in unfounded conspiracies may amplify fear and anxiety, making it difficult for authorities to communicate calm, measured responses and guide the public towards constructive actions.

2. **Resistance to Protective Measures:** Conspiracy-driven skepticism may lead individuals to resist or reject protective measures recommended by authorities during a crisis. This

resistance can range from avoiding evacuation orders to refusing to adhere to public health guidelines, undermining efforts to safeguard public safety.

3. **Spread of Misinformation:** Conspiracy theories often involve the spread of misinformation, which can impede the dissemination of accurate crisis-related information. Individuals influenced by conspiracies may share false narratives, creating confusion and hindering the effectiveness of official communication channels.

4. **Undermining Trust in Authorities:** Belief in conspiracies can erode trust in government agencies, emergency responders, and other authorities crucial for crisis management. This lack of trust can hinder public cooperation, delay responses, and contribute to an atmosphere of uncertainty.

5. **Diversion of Resources:** Efforts to address and debunk conspiracy theories during a crisis can divert resources away from critical response activities. Authorities may find themselves allocating time and resources to counteracting misinformation

rather than focusing on essential crisis response measures.

6. **Delayed Evacuations:** In situations requiring evacuations, belief in conspiracies can lead to delays as individuals question the legitimacy of evacuation orders. This hesitation may result in individuals staying in potentially dangerous locations for longer than necessary, jeopardizing their safety and complicating evacuation efforts.

7. **Challenges for Healthcare Professionals:** Healthcare professionals may face challenges when dealing with patients who

adhere to conspiracy theories, particularly during health crises. Individuals may refuse medical interventions or preventive measures, impacting the effectiveness of healthcare responses.

8. **Discrediting Scientific Guidance:** Conspiracy theories often challenge scientific consensus and evidence-based guidance. This discrediting of scientific advice can lead individuals to dismiss crucial recommendations from experts, hindering the ability to make informed decisions based on reliable information.

9. **Social Discord:** Belief in conspiracies can contribute to social discord during crises. Divisive narratives may pit individuals or groups against each other, making it difficult to foster a sense of unity and collective responsibility needed for effective crisis response.

10. **Exacerbation of Economic Impact:** The spread of conspiracies during crises can exacerbate economic consequences. Misinformation about the causes or solutions to a crisis may lead to irrational economic behaviors, such as panic

buying or market instability, further complicating recovery efforts.

Addressing the impact of conspiracy beliefs on crisis response requires a multi-pronged approach. This includes proactive communication strategies, public education on media literacy, and efforts to build and maintain trust in authorities. Ensuring that accurate information is readily accessible and countering misinformation is crucial for effective crisis management.

15

Conspiracy theories play a significant role in contributing to cultural and social polarization by reinforcing existing biases and creating ideological echo chambers. The proliferation of these theories can deepen divisions within society, fostering an environment where individuals are more likely to be entrenched in their beliefs and less open to opposing viewpoints. Here's how conspiracy theories contribute to cultural and social polarization:

1. **Confirmation Bias:** Conspiracy theories often resonate with individuals who already hold certain beliefs or suspicions.

People are more likely to accept information that confirms their existing views, leading to the reinforcement of confirmation bias. This reinforcement solidifies pre-existing opinions and makes individuals less receptive to alternative perspectives.

2. **Creation of In-Group vs. Out-Group Mentality:** Conspiracy theories can create a sense of belonging among those who subscribe to a particular narrative, forming an in-group. Those who reject or question the conspiracy may be perceived as part of an out-group. This division fosters an "us versus them"

mentality, contributing to social polarization.

3. **Echo Chambers in Online Spaces:** Social media and online platforms play a crucial role in the dissemination of conspiracy theories. Algorithms that prioritize content based on users' preferences can create echo chambers where individuals are exposed to information that aligns with their existing beliefs. This isolation from diverse perspectives reinforces polarization.

4. **Selective Exposure:** Individuals tend to seek

information that aligns with their beliefs and avoid dissenting opinions. The selective exposure to information that supports conspiratorial views intensifies polarization, as individuals become more insulated from alternative viewpoints and less willing to engage in constructive dialogue.

5. **Distrust in Mainstream Institutions:** Conspiracy theories often involve narratives that challenge the legitimacy of mainstream institutions, including the media, government, and scientific organizations. The resulting distrust in these

institutions contributes to the polarization of society, as individuals may turn to alternative sources that reinforce their conspiratorial beliefs.

6. **Political Polarization:** Conspiracy theories frequently intersect with political ideologies, contributing to political polarization. The association of certain conspiracy narratives with specific political views can deepen divisions, making it challenging for individuals to find common ground on important issues.

7. **Normalization of Extreme Views:** The acceptance of conspiracy theories can normalize extreme views within certain communities. This normalization reinforces polarization by making more extreme beliefs and ideologies socially acceptable within specific circles.

8. **Adversarial Political Discourse:** The prevalence of conspiracy theories can contribute to adversarial political discourse. When individuals are convinced that powerful entities are conspiring against them, it can lead to a more confrontational approach to political discussions,

further dividing communities along ideological lines.

9. **Diminished Trust in Expertise:** Conspiracies often involve skepticism toward expert opinions and established knowledge. This distrust in expertise can polarize society by undermining the credibility of scientists, researchers, and other authorities, hindering evidence-based decision-making.

10. **Impact on Social Harmony:** The cultural and social polarization fueled by conspiracy theories can erode social harmony. When individuals

are divided along ideological lines, it becomes challenging to foster a sense of unity and collective responsibility needed for addressing shared challenges and promoting the well-being of society.

Addressing cultural and social polarization requires efforts to promote media literacy, critical thinking, and open dialogue. Encouraging exposure to diverse perspectives, fostering empathy, and building bridges between communities are essential for mitigating the impact of conspiracy theories on social cohesion.

16

Misguided beliefs fueled by conspiracy theories can have a significant economic impact by influencing individuals' decisions, market behaviors, and overall financial stability. These beliefs may lead to irrational economic decisions, market volatility, and a lack of trust in economic institutions. Here's how conspiracy theories can affect the economy:

1. **Market Volatility:** Conspiracy theories can contribute to market volatility as

individuals react to perceived threats or hidden agendas. Believers in certain conspiracies may make impulsive investment decisions based on misinformation, leading to erratic market movements and increased volatility.

2. **Impact on Investor Confidence:** Widespread belief in conspiracy theories can erode investor confidence. Investors may become hesitant to participate in financial markets, fearing manipulation or hidden agendas. This lack of confidence can lead to reduced investment,

slower economic growth, and increased market uncertainty.

3. **Misallocation of Resources:** Economic decisions influenced by conspiracy theories may result in the misallocation of resources. If individuals and businesses base their decisions on unfounded beliefs, they may invest in areas that are not economically viable, leading to inefficiencies and potential economic losses.

4. **Consumer Behavior Changes:** Consumer behavior is often influenced by perceptions and beliefs. Conspiracy theories

can shape consumer attitudes and decisions, affecting spending patterns. If consumers alter their behavior based on false information, it can impact industries and businesses, leading to economic repercussions.

5. **Impact on Global Trade:** Belief in certain conspiracy theories can affect international relations and trade. Misguided perceptions about economic partners may lead to protectionist policies, trade tensions, and disruptions in global supply chains, impacting economic stability on a global scale.

6. **Undermining Government Economic Policies:** Conspiracy theories that target government economic policies may undermine their effectiveness. If a significant portion of the population doubts the legitimacy of economic measures, it can hinder the successful implementation of policies aimed at stabilizing and stimulating the economy.

7. **Reduced Foreign Direct Investment (FDI):** A climate of mistrust fueled by conspiracy theories may deter foreign investors. The perception of economic instability or hidden agendas may discourage foreign

direct investment, limiting the inflow of capital essential for economic development.

8. **Market Manipulation Concerns:** Belief in financial conspiracy theories, such as market manipulation by powerful entities, can lead to concerns about the integrity of financial markets. Investors may fear that markets are rigged against them, leading to a loss of trust and reduced participation.

9. **Impact on Currency Values:** Conspiracy theories can influence perceptions of currency values. If individuals

believe in unfounded currency-related conspiracies, it may lead to speculative actions that impact exchange rates, potentially causing fluctuations in currency values and affecting international trade.

10. **Disruption in Business Operations:** Businesses may be adversely affected by conspiracy-driven actions or decisions. For example, false beliefs about certain industries or businesses could lead to boycotts, protests, or regulatory challenges, disrupting normal business operations and impacting economic stability.

Addressing the economic impact of conspiracy theories requires efforts to promote financial literacy, critical thinking, and transparent communication. Governments, financial institutions, and educators play a crucial role in countering misinformation and fostering an environment where economic decisions are based on accurate information and sound reasoning.

17

The preoccupation with conspiracy theories has the potential to divert attention away from pressing social, economic, and environmental challenges that demand collective action. The focus on imagined or exaggerated threats posed by conspiracies can hinder efforts to address real-world issues that require attention and solutions. Here's how the distraction from genuine issues occurs:

1. **Misallocation of Attention and Resources:** Conspiracy theories often capture public attention, leading to a misallocation of resources and efforts. The energy and resources that could be directed toward addressing tangible issues may instead be consumed by

debunking unfounded claims or countering misinformation.

2. **Undermining Public Discourse:** The prevalence of conspiracy theories can contribute to a decline in substantive public discourse. Instead of engaging in discussions about evidence-based policies and solutions, conversations may become dominated by divisive narratives and unproductive debates, hindering the ability to address genuine issues.

3. **Diverting Political Agendas:** The focus on conspiracy theories can divert

political agendas from addressing critical challenges. Policymakers may find themselves responding to perceived threats rather than focusing on formulating and implementing policies that address issues such as poverty, inequality, or environmental sustainability.

4. **Delay in Problem Solving:** The distraction caused by conspiracy theories can lead to delays in addressing urgent problems. Whether it be a public health crisis, environmental disaster, or economic downturn, the diversion of attention can

impede timely and effective problem-solving.

5. **Erosion of Trust in Institutions:** The perpetuation of conspiracy theories often involves a narrative that questions the legitimacy of institutions. This erosion of trust in key societal entities can hinder cooperation and collaboration, essential elements for addressing complex challenges that require collective efforts.

6. **Disengagement from Civic Responsibilities:** Belief in certain conspiracies may lead individuals to disengage from

civic responsibilities. If people perceive that powerful forces control events regardless of their actions, they may feel powerless and less inclined to participate in community or political activities that could drive positive change.

7. **Impact on Social Activism:** The distraction caused by conspiracy theories may divert attention away from social activism and advocacy for genuine causes. Individuals and groups passionate about specific issues may find their efforts overshadowed by the sensationalism of conspiracies.

8. **Diminished Public Awareness:** The emphasis on conspiracies can diminish public awareness of real challenges. Individuals may become so absorbed in unraveling supposed hidden truths that they lose sight of issues such as climate change, social justice, or economic inequality that require sustained attention and action.

9. **Creation of False Narratives:** Conspiracy theories often involve the creation of false narratives that capture public imagination. These false narratives may overshadow the true stories of societal challenges,

preventing the public from fully understanding and engaging with the complexity of real-world issues.

10. **Polarization and Fragmentation:** The focus on conspiracies can contribute to polarization and fragmentation within society. As individuals become entrenched in their beliefs, divisions may deepen, making it more challenging to foster collective action and cooperation on issues that impact communities as a whole.

Addressing the distraction from genuine issues necessitates efforts to promote critical thinking, media literacy, and a focus on evidence-based decision-making. Encouraging open dialogue, emphasizing the importance of civic engagement, and redirecting public attention toward real challenges are essential for fostering a society that addresses its most pressing concerns.

18

Conspiracy theories that challenge well-established scientific principles have the potential to erode public trust in scientific endeavors. When individuals doubt the legitimacy of widely accepted scientific knowledge, it can have far-reaching consequences on public perception, decision-making, and societal progress. Here's how the dissemination of such conspiracy theories diminishes scientific trust:

1. **Discrediting Established Research:** Conspiracy theories often attempt to discredit well-established scientific research by casting doubt on the methodologies, motives, or findings of reputable scientists. This concerted effort to undermine the credibility of scientific endeavors contributes to

a climate of skepticism and mistrust.

2. **Fostering Distrust in Scientific Institutions:** Conspiracies may target scientific institutions, portraying them as part of an alleged plot or cover-up. This portrayal can lead to a widespread distrust in institutions such as universities, research organizations, and governmental agencies that are pivotal in advancing scientific knowledge.

3. **Promoting Anti-Intellectualism:** Conspiracies challenging scientific principles can contribute to a broader anti-

intellectual sentiment. This skepticism may extend beyond specific scientific theories to a general distrust of intellectual pursuits, hindering the acceptance of evidence-based decision-making.

4. **Undermining Public Health Efforts:** In the context of public health, conspiracy theories can undermine efforts to address pandemics or vaccination campaigns. Doubt in scientific consensus can lead to vaccine hesitancy, compromising public health initiatives and jeopardizing disease prevention.

5. **Resistance to Technological Advances:** Conspiracy theories that question the safety or necessity of certain technologies can foster resistance to technological advancements. This resistance may impede progress in areas such as renewable energy, medical innovation, and other fields crucial for societal development.

6. **Creation of Parallel Scientific Narratives:** Conspiracies often involve the promotion of alternative scientific narratives that lack empirical support. This parallel narrative-building can lead to the existence

of competing, unfounded scientific claims, further confusing the public and eroding trust in well-established scientific knowledge.

7. **Discouraging Scientific Inquiry:** When conspiracy theories discourage trust in scientific findings, individuals may become hesitant to pursue scientific careers or engage in research. This discouragement of scientific inquiry can impede advancements in knowledge and innovation.

8. **Cherry-Picking Anomalies:** Conspiracies often

rely on the selective highlighting of anomalies or uncertainties within scientific fields. By emphasizing isolated instances where scientific understanding is evolving or incomplete, conspiracies create a distorted image of the scientific process, fostering mistrust.

9. **Polarizing Public Opinion:** Conspiracy theories challenging scientific principles can polarize public opinion, creating divisions between those who accept mainstream scientific consensus and those who adhere to alternative views. This polarization hampers constructive

dialogue and collaboration on addressing shared challenges.

10. **Delay in Policy Implementation:** Skepticism toward well-established scientific principles can lead to delays in the implementation of policies informed by scientific evidence. This delay may hinder responses to environmental concerns, public health crises, or other issues requiring evidence-based decision-making.

Addressing the diminished trust in science requires proactive efforts to communicate scientific findings transparently, promote science literacy, and build bridges between scientific communities and the broader public. Encouraging critical thinking and emphasizing the rigorous, self-correcting nature of the scientific process are crucial for fostering a society that values and trusts scientific endeavors.

19

Belief in certain global conspiracy theories has the potential to impede international cooperation on critical issues such as climate change, public health, and other global challenges. When individuals or nations are influenced by unfounded suspicions of hidden agendas or malevolent plots, it can hinder collaborative efforts to address shared problems. Here's how global cooperation can be hindered by the influence of global conspiracy theories:

1. **Undermining Trust in International Institutions:** Global conspiracy theories often involve the portrayal of international institutions, such as the United Nations or international health organizations, as part of an alleged global plot. This portrayal erodes trust in these institutions, hindering their

effectiveness as facilitators of global cooperation.

2. **Creation of Mistrust between Nations:** Belief in global conspiracies may lead to mistrust between nations. Countries may be hesitant to collaborate with one another if they perceive hidden motives or manipulation by other nations, impeding diplomatic efforts and the development of international partnerships.

3. **Diverting Attention from Shared Challenges:** The focus on global conspiracy theories can divert attention away from shared challenges that require collective

action. Instead of addressing issues like climate change or global health crises, nations may become preoccupied with perceived threats that have little basis in reality.

4. **Nationalistic Responses:** Belief in global conspiracies can foster a nationalistic mindset where countries prioritize their perceived interests over collaborative solutions. This mentality may hinder the development of international agreements and cooperation frameworks needed to tackle global issues collectively.

5. **Impeding Information Sharing:** Conspiracies often involve skepticism about information coming from other nations. This skepticism may impede the sharing of critical data and information needed for collaborative responses to global challenges, hindering the effectiveness of international cooperation.

6. **Resistance to Global Agreements:** Nations influenced by global conspiracy theories may resist participating in global agreements or treaties. This resistance can lead to the breakdown of collaborative

efforts, especially in areas where collective action is essential for meaningful impact.

7. **Delaying Joint Efforts:** Belief in global conspiracies can contribute to delays in initiating joint efforts to address urgent global issues. Nations may hesitate to take coordinated action if they suspect hidden motives or are influenced by conspiracy-driven skepticism.

8. **Fueling Tensions and Conflicts:** The influence of global conspiracy theories can contribute to heightened tensions and conflicts between nations.

The suspicion and mistrust fueled by conspiratorial thinking may escalate geopolitical disputes, making it challenging to foster diplomatic solutions.

9. **Compromising Global Health Initiatives:** In the context of public health, belief in global health conspiracies can hinder international efforts to combat pandemics. Cooperation in vaccine distribution, information sharing, and coordinated responses may be compromised, affecting the effectiveness of global health initiatives.

10. **Erosion of Diplomatic Relations:** The influence of global conspiracy theories can erode diplomatic relations between nations. If countries are suspicious of each other's motives, it becomes difficult to build the trust necessary for effective collaboration on global challenges.

Addressing the hindrance to global cooperation necessitates efforts to counter misinformation, promote diplomatic dialogue, and foster a shared understanding of the importance of collective action. Emphasizing the benefits of international collaboration and building trust between nations are essential for overcoming the challenges posed by global conspiracy beliefs.

20

The adoption of conspiracy beliefs can contribute to psychological stress, both at the individual and societal levels. The constant suspicion, fear, and uncertainty associated with conspiratorial thinking can have detrimental effects on mental well-being. Here's how conspiracy beliefs may lead to psychological stress:

1. **Chronic Uncertainty:**
Conspiracy theories often thrive
on uncertainty, promoting
narratives that suggest hidden
motives and undisclosed
information. The chronic
uncertainty created by these
beliefs can contribute to
heightened stress levels as
individuals grapple with perceived
threats and unanswered questions.

2. **Loss of Control:**
Conspiracy beliefs often depict a
world where powerful entities
control events behind the scenes.
The sense of powerlessness and
loss of control over one's
circumstances can be a significant

source of stress, impacting individuals' mental health and overall sense of well-being.

3. **Heightened Anxiety:** The narratives surrounding conspiracy theories often involve potential threats or impending disasters. This can lead to heightened anxiety as individuals internalize and ruminate on the perceived dangers, even when there is no credible evidence supporting the conspiratorial claims.

4. **Social Isolation:** Belief in certain conspiracy theories may lead to social isolation. Individuals who hold

unconventional or extreme beliefs may find it challenging to connect with others who do not share their views, contributing to feelings of alienation and stress.

5. **Fear of Persecution:** Some conspiracy theories involve the perception of persecution by powerful entities. The fear of being targeted or persecuted for one's beliefs can create a constant state of anxiety, leading to stress-related mental health issues.

6. **Interpersonal Strain:** Conspiracy beliefs can strain interpersonal relationships. Friends and family members may

find it challenging to engage with individuals who hold extreme or divisive views, leading to increased social conflict and stress.

7. **Cognitive Dissonance:** Individuals who subscribe to conspiracy theories may experience cognitive dissonance when confronted with evidence that contradicts their beliefs. This internal conflict can contribute to stress as individuals grapple with the challenge of reconciling conflicting information.

8. **Impact on Decision-Making:** The influence of

conspiracy beliefs can impact decision-making processes. Individuals may make decisions based on unfounded fears or suspicions, leading to stress if these decisions have negative consequences for their well-being or the well-being of others.

9. **Escalation of Hypervigilancc:** Conspiracy beliefs often promote hypervigilance, where individuals are constantly on alert for perceived threats. This heightened state of vigilance can lead to chronic stress, as the mind and body are continuously on edge in anticipation of potential dangers.

10. **Reduced Coping Mechanisms:** Belief in conspiracies may reduce the effectiveness of traditional coping mechanisms. Individuals may be less likely to seek social support, engage in stress-reducing activities, or adopt healthy coping strategies when their worldview is dominated by suspicion and fear.

On a societal level, the collective adoption of conspiracy beliefs can contribute to a culture of mistrust, anxiety, and division. Addressing the psychological stress associated with conspiracy beliefs requires a multifaceted approach that includes promoting critical thinking, fostering open dialogue, and providing mental health resources and support for individuals grappling with the psychological impact of these beliefs.